Held Back From God's Best
It's the Small Things that Make the Difference

Rev. William Kimando

AuthorHouse™
1663 Liberty Drive, Suite 200
Bloomington, IN 47403
www.authorhouse.com
Phone: 1-800-839-8640

© 2008 Rev. William Kimando. All rights reserved.

No part of this book may be reproduced, stored in a retrieval system, or transmitted by any means without the written permission of the author.

First published by AuthorHouse 4/11/2008

ISBN: 978-1-4343-5899-8 (sc)

Printed in the United States of America
Bloomington, Indiana

This book is printed on acid-free paper.

Redemption Faith Living Ministries Int'l, Toronto, Ontario, Canada

Dedication

This book is dedicated to Jayne, who has demonstrated what faith is really about by standing together with me in some of my fieriest battles. I love you for your sincerity and commitment and I am blessed to have you in my life.

And to Edgar, thank you for having me as your student where you have taught me how to be patient, just as God is patient with us. You are special to me.

Contents

Dedication v

Acknowledgements ix

Introduction xiii

Chapter 1 – Does God Really Love Me? 1

Chapter 2 – The Intergrity of Our Words 5

Chapter 3 – The Guilt of The Past 8

Chapter 4 – Failure to Understand
                the Promises 13

Chapter 5 – Failure to Understand
                Our Responsibility 17

Chapter 6 – Lack of Faith 24

Chapter 7 – Lack Of Patience 31

Chapter 8 – Complaining and Grumbling ... 39

Chapter 9 – The Starting Point 46

Acknowledgements

There are people that God sends into our lives at the right place and at the right time. These people are sent as God's sign posts to point us to where we ought to go, when we get lost in hopelessness and despair.

Special thanks to Sherri Hackwell, your passion for God motivated you to devote many precious hours editing this book to make sure the message of the gospel would not be compromised. God alone is the only one who can repay you.

To the members of our Ministry who believed in my calling and have supported our vision, thank you. Your prayers and support during the most trying times of this ministry gave me strength to go on preaching the gospel of Jesus Christ.

Mrs. Minnie Mungai, a woman who sees people as God sees them. Thank you for believing in me when most people had written me off and turned their backs on me. I can never thank you enough for the many times you reached out to me and cheered me on to stand up and fight the good fight of faith.

Mrs. Murage, you taught me the meaning of the love of God. I thank you for sharing with me Dr. Jerry Savelle's tapes. These tapes changed and altered the course of my life.

Mr & Mrs. Mburu, words fail me in expressing my gratitude. This book and my ministry are a product of the seed you sowed in my life, when I desperately needed it. God alone is the only one who can ever repay you.

Dr. Jerry Savelle, thank you for listening to Mrs. Savelle's prophecy and preaching the gospel to Africa. You caused me to love being a Christian, and molded me to be a servant of the Most High. The teaching I received from JSMI Bible Institute was invaluable. I don't think I could ever have learned these truths anywhere else. You opened your heart and shared Jesus in reality. Through you, I am living my calling and I say thank you.

Bishop C. Lloyd Battiestte, you are a true man of God. I have never had to book an appointment to see you despite your very busy schedule. Any time I need your counsel, you are always available. Thank you for incubating our ministry, tending and nourishing us to make sure we are safe and growing healthy. Your love for God and people greatly enriches the Kingdom of God. May God take you to places you never imagined possible because of your desire to make the dreams of many saints become possible.

Finally to the friends and partners of our ministry, your consistent support has given us strength to keep doing what God has called us to do. Thank you.

Introduction

I came to the Lord at a time when I was feeling frustrated and empty. Although at the time I was a successful businessman, I was tired of the tricks and methods that I had to apply to stay in the game.

Every day, I would wake up and lay out the plans and even deception that I saw as necessary for me to get as much profit as I could. This was hard and fruitless work.

One day, my friend invited me to her church. For me, it was the first time I heard the gospel message. I heard that Jesus loved me, and He would take care of my pain and struggles. And believe me, there were many of both! After attending services a couple of times in that church, the Word of God began to work in me, convicting me and bringing me to a place of repentance. Finally, I became so painfully aware of the emptiness of my life, and how far away I was from God, and I began to yearn for this love that made Christ willing to die on the Cross—for me. And one day in 1993, I walked down the aisle and I accepted Jesus as my Lord and Savior.

I did not make this decision just to escape hell, I also needed relief from my struggles, and from the frustrations and failures of this life; my earthly existence desperately needed the Lord's help! I wanted someone else to take care of me. I felt completely exhausted from trying to do it all on my own.

As a young believer, my prayers seemed to get answered almost immediately. And this got me excited. But just like school, where things become tougher with every passing grade, things began to change for me as I matured in my walk with the Lord. I came to discover something I had not been prepared for. Some of my prayers began to take a bit longer to manifest. Sometimes instead of seeing the quick results I had become accustomed to, it would take weeks, months, and even years to see the answers. I realized I had joined the good fight of faith that the Apostle Paul wrote to Timothy about in 1 Timothy 6:12,

> "*Fight the good fight of faith, lay hold on eternal life, to which you were also called and have confessed the good confession in the presence of many witnesses*".

In my ten years of ministry, I have often come across believers who have told me how weary they are of fighting. They have told me they are tired of always being on the defensive. Why, they wonder, must they always seem to have to wait for so long for things that it appears other believers and even non-believers receive almost instantly? We have all been there. "Why me, Lord"?

These questions from sincere Christians started a quest for me. I wanted to know what it was that could be responsible for the delay in the manifestation of our prayers.

In this book I will address some of the obstacles that we face in our human limitations that may deny or delay our blessings from manifesting as realities.

It is my prayer that this book will shed some light in some of the areas where we may have been dropping the ball.

Chapter 1

Does God Really Love Me?

The LORD appeared to us in the past, saying: "I have loved you with an everlasting love; I have drawn you with loving-kindness".
                                    Jeremiah 31: 3

We are living at a time when relationships are breaking down at the drop of a hat. These relationship breakdowns end up leaving a trail of broken and wounded hearts in their wake. Many people are walking around wounded and shy to commit to relationships because they fear they will be hurt again.

When we read in Jeremiah 31:3 that God loves us with an everlasting love, our mind, like a huge database begins to search for a good reason why God would be interested in loving us. We fail to understand how God could love us when He is well aware of all the messes we have made with our past relationships. Why would He want a relationship with us?

And then we read 1 John 3:1, which says, "*How great is the love the Father has lavished on us, that we should be called children of God! And that is what we are!*" Reading this verse, we begin to have some insight into this love of God. But the word "Father" in this scripture, takes our mind on a journey to remind us how the father figures in our lives treated us. We try to reconcile the scriptures with the reality of how we were treated by these fathers. And from this point we approach God.

Our past relationship with our father figures will have a great influence on how easily we accept that God the Father does truly love us.

I was born at a time when my father was trying to build his own business. His line of business required him to leave early in the morning and come back home late at night. And by the time he got home in the evening, he was too tired to give us any quality time. At that time, according to the African culture, a man had little to do with the upbringing of the children. It was the mother's responsibility to bring up children while the father's role was to make sure the children were provided for. My father did an awesome job as a provider and we never lacked in anything. But spending time with us did not come easily. The only time we got to spend any time with him was when he took us for a movie perhaps once a year, or when we wanted him to buy us something. The other times were when he administered punishment after our mother had reported our mistakes to him. I never heard him tell me that he loved me at any one time. But I thank God my father is now born again and spreading the gospel, and we have a wonderful relationship.

Given my past relationship with my earthly father, I could not understand how God—the Creator of heaven and earth—our heavenly Father, could say He loved me. I assumed that I needed to do something to earn His love. This left me to assume that anytime I prayed, my answer was dependent on what I had done or not done. I kept thinking back to the sins I had committed, and believe me, out of those thoughts, I wouldn't expect much from my prayers.

I didn't know 1 John 1:9, *"If we confess our sins, he is faithful and just to forgive us our sins and to cleanse us from all unrighteousness*". Thank God for His Word! If you feel convicted about any sin in your life, and you are a believer, confess your sins and believe that you have been forgiven according to God's Word in 1 John 1:9.

Sometimes we confess our sins, but then we have a hard time believing we have actually been forgiven. We should not only believe that God has forgiven us, but we should also forgive ourselves.

But this forgiveness and acceptance can only happen if we are fully convinced of the fact that God loves us unconditionally. We have to know that God is not looking at our flaws to measure how much He will love us. God loves you and me the same way He loves our Lord Jesus Christ. How do I know this? Jesus said it Himself! "*As the Father hath loved me, so have I loved you: continue ye in my love*" (John 15:9). God loves Jesus and us with the same love! He may not be pleased with some of the things that we do, but His love for us does not and will not change—ever.

Chapter 2

The Intergrity of Our Words

"God is not a man, that He should lie; neither the son of man, that He should repent. Hath he said, and shall he not do it? or hath he spoken, and shall he not make it good?"
                               Numbers 23:19

Sometimes we have situations where a person who promised to love us forever has ended up hurting us really badly. We can end up hurt by someone that we loved, someone we gave our hearts and trust to, who said what they did not mean, simply because they wanted to use us or to manipulate us.

Perhaps you are a woman who sacrificed her youth, career and life to marry your high school sweetheart because he told you he loved you. But after a few years maybe the love that you were promised turned into regular sessions of abuse, and eventually he walked out on you—or you found yourself forced to leave your family home for your safety or the safety and security of your children.

Jobless and without a career or support network, you were left bitter and with children to care for. You vowed never again to allow anybody to hurt you or your children. And with this background, you were told that God loves you and He wants a relationship with you. He wants to carry the burden for you.

Our past experiences, good or bad, will always influence how seriously we are willing to take other people's words. For example, if you had parents who constantly re-affirmed their love for you and demonstrated their love to you with how they treated you while you were growing up, you will be more easily convinced that God loves you.

But if your parents or spouse rejected you, that spirit of rejection will hinder you in accepting the fact that God loves you. And if you don't believe God loves you, then you will not be able to believe anything else He has promised you. We need to remember that God is not a man that He should lie. The Word of God says in Romans 5:8, "*But God demonstrates His own love toward us, in that while we were still sinners, Christ died for us*" (NKJV). God does not only promise to love you, He already does, and He has proven it in His willingness to sacrifice His own Son for an opportunity to have a love relationship with you. If you were hurt in your past relationships, and you have been having a hard time receiving God's love, I want you to take a moment and ask the Lord to help you to forgive those who have hurt you, and allow the Lord to heal your wounded heart. You will find out that the more you give in to God, the more secure you will feel. You can trust Him. Our God is dependable and trustworthy.

Chapter 3

The Guilt of The Past

"Come now, let us reason together," says the LORD. "Though your sins are like scarlet, they shall be as white as snow; though they are red as crimson, they shall be like wool".

Isaiah 1:18

If we are not careful, our past has a way of sneaking up on us. We will find past failures speaking to us about how unworthy we are. This reminds us of all the horrible stuff we did before we came to the Lord, and we feel like we do not deserve God's love. It becomes difficult for some people to accept or to believe that God can forgive our sins and love us, despite our past sins and mistakes.

Sometimes, we may have committed what we consider to be terrible sins and we walk around punishing ourselves by remaining conscious of what we did, despite the fact that we may believe that we have been forgiven. We may assume that others will find out what we did before we came to the Lord and they will no longer like or accept us. We build walls around ourselves, not allowing anybody into our hearts, believing we are protecting ourselves from future hurts. Many have walked this way for years, full of guilt and shame. Perhaps you have found yourself doing this—keeping barriers up to keep the pain out. But what we're really doing is keeping the pain in. Not wanting to appear as a less than perfect Christian can stop us from opening up and being real with those around us—and with God.

And it is in this closed condition that we approach God, feeling like we are supposed to pay for our sins for the rest of our lives. Whenever we face a challenge, be it financial lack, sickness, or any demonic attack, instead of praying and believing for our victory, we can find ourselves accepting the current situation as a punishment of our past sins. I am not saying that there are no consequences for sin, but when God forgives you, He remembers your sins no more. The only accepted payment for sin is death. The Bible says so in Ezekiel 18:20, "*The soul that sinneth, it shall die*" (KJV).

This is a debt, quite simply, that no human being could ever afford to pay. But Jesus freely paid it for me and for you. So accept it; receive it. It's time to forgive and forget those old sins. Stop beating yourself up over a debt that was supernaturally paid off two thousand years ago!

These and many other experiences greatly contribute to our perverted perception of life, and can hinder our ability to love and to be loved by God. We must understand that God's love is not subject to what we do, or have done, or what we will do. God loves us with an everlasting love. God's love is unconditional. And God's love was demonstrated in the death of His own Son as clearly stated in Romans 5:8, "*But God demonstrates His own love toward us, in that while we were still sinners, Christ died for us*".

Jesus did not die for us after we got cleaned up. Not after we became holy and perfect. It was when we were yet sinners. He died for us when we were still rebellious; He chose to die for us when we were still being abused and rejected, when we were still doing drugs.

He died for us when we were still struggling with addictions and lies. He died for us when we were still complete and utter failures. And although other people may have looked at you and written you off, Jesus looked at you and said, "I love you, and you are worth dying for."

God loves you *(Yes, you, the one who is reading this book!)*. He loves you with an everlasting love. Let that settle in your spirit. If you have received Jesus as your Lord and Savior, then your sins are forgiven. You have received the spirit of adoption and God has become your Father. God Himself is telling you, "I love you and I will never leave you nor forsake you. My thoughts of you are for good not for evil to give you a hope and a future. I don't think evil of you" (Jeremiah 29:11, author's paraphrase). God is not sitting in heaven with a baseball bat waiting for you to make a mistake so He can swat your head. The Word of God says, *"For the eyes of the LORD run to and fro throughout the whole earth, to shew himself strong in the behalf of them whose heart is perfect toward him"* (2 Chronicles 16:9). You see, God is looking to bless us, not to harm us!

When we allow this fact to settle in our spirit, our faith will begin to grow, and we will find it easier to believe that God not only *can* love us, but that He *does* love us. As the scripture says, "*Now faith is the substance of things hoped for, the evidence of things not seen*" (Hebrews 11:1). We must be convinced that God has every intention of answering our prayers. Only when we are convinced will we be able to demonstrate the evidence of our faith. But the only way we can be convinced that God will bless us is by knowing His promises in regard to our needs.

Chapter 4

Failure to Understand the Promises

My people are destroyed for lack of knowledge. Because you have rejected knowledge, I also will reject you from being priest for Me; Because you have forgotten the law of your God, I also will forget your children.

Hosea 4:6

When you buy an item from the store, it comes with a purchaser's contract. Normally, this contract is written in complicated language, in very small print, that would typically discourage the buyer from reading through it. This contract is where the seller outlines the warranty on the product, and the liability coverage, just in case your product becomes defective. Since most customers don't bother to read the contract until the item they've bought develops a problem, they get a shock when their claim is turned down. Had they bothered to read the fine print, they would have been aware of what was covered in the warranty before they purchased the product. But their lack of knowledge does not change the limitations of the manufacturer's warranty.

Likewise, as believers we have a tendency to not read the Bible in order to understand what God has promised us. Then we walk around expecting something that God has not promised. And when things don't turn out the way we expect, we become upset and angry with God.

In other situations, we may read the Scriptures, but we end up misinterpreting them to validate what we want to do rather than what God has promised. "God, I want a spouse, but I want this certain one who is already married, because I don't think the spouse they have now makes them happy." And after such a prayer, we begin to help God with the answer. But our misuse of the Scriptures will not change what God has promised, and instead, we will end up being hurt and hurting other people in the process.

But, like a purchase contract, misquoting scriptures will not produce the manifestation of your expectation. God said in Psalm 89:34, "*My covenant I will not break, nor alter the word that has gone out of My lips*". Therefore, to be able to hold God to His Word, we must clearly know and understand what He has promised, as well as rightfully interpreting His Word. Paul told Timothy in 2 Timothy 2:15, "*Study to shew thyself approved unto God, a workman that needeth not to be ashamed, rightly dividing the word of truth*" (KJV).

Why is this so important? Because your faith and confidence in God depends on how clearly you understand the promises of God concerning your situation. If you were to get stuck in a storm, and you called your friend for help, but your phone battery died before your friend could tell you he was coming, how confident would you be that help was on the way? My guess is that from that time on, every sound of a vehicle that you heard, you would be expecting to see your friend. But with every passing minute, you would begin to get more and more anxious and afraid that you were stuck without help. You might even begin to think that perhaps they weren't coming after all, for one reason or another. You've lost your confidence, simply because you don't know for sure what has been promised.

The Apostle Paul says in Philippians 4:6-7, *"Be anxious for nothing, but in everything by prayer and supplication, with thanksgiving, let your requests be made known to God; and the peace of God, which surpasses all understanding, will guard your hearts and minds through Christ Jesus"*.

Why do you have peace? Because you are convinced that God is able—and willing—to do as He has promised. Your trust in God will cast away all fear and your heart will receive the comfort of His peace. But unless we know for sure what God has promised, our expectancy will be shaky at best.

We must desire to know Him and the power of His resurrection, as stated in Philippians 3:10, and we must we willing to search His Word diligently so we can be assured of His promises to us.

Chapter 5

Failure to Understand Our Responsibility

Now the LORD had said to Abram: "Get out of your country, From your family And from your father's house, To a land that I will show you. I will make you a great nation; I will bless you And make your name great; And you shall be a blessing. I will bless those who bless you, And I will curse him who curses you; And in you all the families of the earth shall be blessed."

Genesis 12:1-3

When God approached Abram, he told him in Genesis 12:1 to "get out". And then in verse 2 and 3 of that same chapter, God told Abram what He would do for him if he obeyed. Later, after God had changed his name to Abraham and blessed him with the son of promise, he told him again of the promised blessings.

> *Then the Angel of the LORD called to Abraham a second time out of heaven, and said: "By Myself I have sworn, says the LORD, because you have done this thing, and have not withheld your son, your only son—blessing I will bless you, and multiplying I will multiply your descendants as the stars of the heaven and as the sand which is on the seashore; and your descendants shall possess the gate of their enemies. In your seed all the nations of the earth shall be blessed, because you have obeyed My voice." So Abraham returned to his young men, and they rose and went together to Beersheba; and Abraham dwelt at Beersheba*
>
> Genesis 22:15-19

In other words, God was saying, "Abraham, because you have kept your part of the deal, it is now My turn to do what I promised you. Since Abraham had been obedient to do what

God had told Him to do, God could fulfill what He had promised Abraham.

Jesus told us our faith in God would bring His promises to pass in our lives. He said,

> *"Have faith in God. For assuredly, I say to you, whoever says to this mountain, 'Be removed and be cast into the sea,' and does not doubt in his heart, but believes that those things he says will be done, he will have whatever he says. Therefore I say to you, whatever things you ask when you pray, believe that you receive them, and you will have them"*
> Mark 11:22-24.

There is no situation that you will ever encounter that God has not given a promise for. But for every promise given, an action is required from us or an evidence of your faith will be required (see Hebrews 11:1). The Bible also says,

> *"But someone will say, "You have faith, and I have works." Show me your faith without your works, and I will show you my faith by my works. You believe that there is one God. You do well. Even the demons believe—and tremble! But do*

you want to know, O foolish man, that faith without works is dead?"
                                                James 2:18-20

And this faith comes only by hearing, and hearing by the word of God (see Romans 10:17).

God told Joshua that the secret to success was in keeping God's Word before him, clearly understanding and rightfully interpreting it, and knowing what needed to be done—and then following through by doing it! Then and only then, he was told, would he obtain favor and success (see Joshua 1:8, author's paraphrase).

You can buy a very good product, but if you do not understand the instructions on how to use it, you will not enjoy the maximum benefits of that product. When you buy a car, it comes with an owner's manual, which gives you the details of what it can and cannot do, and what benefits it has and doesn't have available. This manual tells you what type of oil to use, what grade of gas to use, etc. But it doesn't matter if the car is old or new, if you don't operate it according to the directions of the manufacturer's manual, you will not receive the full benefits of your car. If the car has a gas engine, and you put diesel instead of gas in the tank, you will ruin the engine. If you fail to do regular service checks, the car soon won't run properly, and it is not the fault of the manual; it is simply your failure to follow the instructions.

Likewise, we must clearly understand God's promises and the role we are required to play to activate the spiritual laws included in the Word. Only when we put understanding and action together can we receive the manifestation of these promises. For example, a common problem I have observed in our churches today is how we are diligent to pray for financial blessings, yet we have a problem with giving. This goes directly against the spiritual principles laid out in the Word. To mention but two scriptures, Malachi 3:8-10 states:

> *"Will a man rob God? yet you have robbed Me! But you say, ' In what way have we robbed You?' In tithes and offerings. You are cursed with a curse, For you have robbed Me, Even this whole nation. Bring all the tithes into the storehouse, That there may be food in My house, And try Me now in this," Says the LORD of hosts, " If I will not open for you the windows of heaven And pour*

out for you such blessing That there will not be room enough to receive it.

And in Luke 6:38 it says,

"Give, and it will be given to you: good measure, pressed down, shaken together, and running over will be put into your bosom. For with the same measure that you use, it will be measured back to you."

If we are to claim these promises, our faith should motivate us to do what the Word of God commands, and then we can expect to receive what God has promised. But claiming the promises without doing what the Word commands is just wishful thinking and not faith. And Hebrews 11:6 says, *"But without faith it is impossible to please Him, for he who comes to God must believe that He is, and that He is a rewarder of those who diligently seek Him"*.

Every promise requires first an action, and faith or fear motivates how we react. If you act in fear, Satan will be commissioned to act, and if you act in faith God will be commissioned to act. Faith and fear are complete opposites!

Remember, you can only expect what you know you have been promised. If we are to expect to receive from God, there is only one way, and that is through Jesus Christ–by faith. Faith is the channel between earth and heaven. The level of your receiving is in direct proportion to your faith.

Chapter 6

Lack of Faith

Now faith is the substance of things hoped for, the evidence of things not seen.

Hebrews 11:1

Nowadays, wherever we turn, we are exposed to all sorts of information, and most of it is contrary to the Scriptures. Information bombards us on how to have safe sex, on smoking and drinking, safe drug use, easy divorce, etc. We are overloaded with messages and knowledge on anything and everything but Jesus. And since we are living in the dispensation of media control, everywhere we turn, we are forced to digest this information whether we like it or not.

It has become okay to discuss sex in our offices, but we cannot talk about Jesus. We can openly talk about and involve people in divination and psychic activities, but we cannot tell them about the Holy Spirit. We can read the horoscopes in the newspaper, and tell people they should believe them, but we cannot tell people about the Word of God that guarantees the outcome of every situation.

We have reached a place in this world where those who desire to walk and live by faith must make a conscious decision, like Joshua, to put the Word of God before them day and night. We must meditate on God's Word, and what the Word says about us and about every situation in our lives, all the time. Whether we are in the field, in the city, at home, or in the office, the Word needs to be first. ONLY then can we expect to enjoy the full benefits of our faith.

David said in Psalm 1 1-3,

> *"Blessed is the man Who walks not in the counsel of the ungodly, Nor stands in the path of sinners, Nor sits in the seat of the scornful; But his delight is in the law of the LORD, And in His law he meditates day and night. He shall be like a tree Planted by the rivers of water,*

*That brings forth its fruit in its season,
Whose leaf also shall not wither; And
whatever he does shall prosper".*

David, one of the greatest kings Israel ever had, reached this conclusion: the Word of God is like rivers of water, which nourishes our lives to bear fruit in every situation.

Friend, our prosperity will only come when we turn our back on the world's way of doing things and delight ourselves in the law of the Lord. Understand me please, when I speak of prosperity I don't mean just money, I mean a healthy life in all spheres. I mean satisfaction and fulfillment in life. Therefore, faith is not measured by what you say, it is measured by what you do, and what you do is dictated by what you believe. That is why we are told in Philippians 4:6-7,

"Be anxious for nothing, but in everything by prayer and supplication, with thanksgiving, let your requests be made known to God; and the peace of God, which surpasses all understanding, will guard your hearts and minds through Christ Jesus".

The peace of God will only guard our hearts when we are convinced that God will do what

He says, and that He is able and willing to do it. This is not easy to believe at first, but the more you get to know Jesus, the easier it will become.

We have to renew our minds as the Apostle Paul encourages us in Romans 12:2, "*And be not conformed to this world: but be ye transformed by the renewing of your mind, that ye may prove what is that good, and acceptable, and perfect, will of God*".

Let me make reference to two scriptures, one in the Old Testament and one in the New Testament, which clearly show how to obtain prosperity and success. First, I'll make reference again to Joshua 1:8,

> "*This Book of the Law shall not depart from your mouth, but you shall meditate in it day and night, that you may observe to do according to all that is written in it. For then you will make your way prosperous, and then you will have good success*".

Secondly, I will remind you of Romans 10:17, "*So then faith comes by hearing, and hearing by the word of God*".

From these two scriptures, it is evident that no matter what era we are living in, the principle of prosperity and success is the same. Whether

God is speaking to Joshua or through the Apostle Paul, the statement is the same. The more we hear and meditate on the Word of God, the more we develop our faith; and the more faith we have, the more prosperous and successful we will be. And then we can enter into a place where we are not anxious for anything, since God's peace will guard our hearts.

Success my friend will not come from:

- How long you fast, although fasting is a necessary discipline in a believer's life.
- Success will not come from how hard you work, although working hard is also important.

A believer's success will be as a result of how much of the Word of God we have in us. It is not how much you know, but it is how much of the Word you believe.

Faith, Hebrews 11:1 says, is evidence. Evidence is something that demonstrates or proves what you are claiming to be true. When you are taken before a judge, it does not matter how much you claim your innocence, without the evidence to prove your claim, you don't stand a chance. But with the evidence supporting your claim, it does not matter what the charges are, your evidence will convince the judge and the jury of your innocence.

The same thing applies to the life of a believer. If we want to receive answers to our prayers, we must approach God by faith. And the only way to have the God kind of faith is by consistently being exposed to the Scriptures.

Remember Mark 11:23-24:

> *For assuredly, I say to you, whoever says to this mountain, 'Be removed and be cast into the sea,' and does not doubt in his heart, but believes that those things he says will be done, he will have whatever he says. Therefore I say to you, whatever things you ask when you pray, believe that you receive them, and you will have them.*

Every promise is conditional upon what we believe. Our faith determines the outcome. So if you would like to see the manifestation you must believe and not doubt in your heart. The Scriptures say in Proverbs 23:7, "*As a man thinketh in his heart, so is he*". Faith is not thinking, "well if Plan A doesn't work out, I've always got Plan B". Faith is Plan A, and Plan A only. This is what faith is all about. It is either God's way or no way. Faith is not praying, "God I will wait for You until three o'clock today, but if You don't answer me, I will move on to plan B". No, faith should be, "God on You alone, I will wait all day long".

"Wait for the Lord; Be strong, and let your heart take courage; Yes, wait for the Lord" (Psalm 27:14).

Sometimes we start out very well. We read the Scriptures, we interpret them rightly, we believe and act on them, but we still fail to receive. Why? Because we quit before we receive our answer. Believers require patience to take them through, all the way from Amen to there it is! It's patience that carries faith through to the expected destination.

Chapter 7

Lack Of Patience

And not only so, but we glory in tribulations also: knowing that tribulation worketh patience; And patience, experience; and experience, hope: And hope maketh not ashamed; because the love of God is shed abroad in our hearts by the Holy Ghost which is given unto us.

Romans 5:3-5

Rest in the LORD, and wait patiently for him: fret not thyself because of him who prospereth in his way, because of the man who bringeth wicked devices to pass.

Psalm 37:7

Successful businesses have a foundation of numerous setbacks, sealed with a layer of patience and persistence. A successful professional is a product of hard work and patience, a person who knows the importance of studying and sitting for the exams in order to become proficient in their chosen field. With every exam, there comes a period of study time just to pass that one exam.

Some people may be tempted to skip the training and decide to obtain fake diplomas or degrees. This will not make them a professional, but it will only make them look like a professional—at least on the outside—on paper only. And there is a big difference between looking like and being.

This outward perception has made many people become envious and impatient. They focus on those who look like they are successful but in reality they are not. Psalm 37:1 in the KJV says, *"Fret not thyself because of evildoers, neither be thou envious against the workers of iniquity."*

If I were to borrow a million dollars, and then go out and buy a big house, a few cars and some expensive clothes, would this make me successful? No, of course not! It would only make me look successful, but in reality I am not, because everything I have is borrowed and I would still be required to pay for it. But if I patiently apply God's principles, pray, and sow seed towards my need, eventually I will be successful. Here's what the Bible says about it:

> *Then Isaac sowed in that land, and reaped in the same year a hundredfold; and the LORD blessed him. The man began to prosper, and continued prospering until he became very prosperous; for he had possessions of flocks and possessions of herds and a great number of servants. So the Philistines envied him.*
> Genesis 26:12-14

> *The blessing of the LORD makes one rich, And He adds no sorrow with it.*
> Proverbs 10:22

That is the kind of success God spoke to Joshua about, which comes as a result of a continuous focus upon the Word, day and night meditation, and the doing of the Word of God. Not a casual glance or casual praying, it is a continuous, persistent focus on God's word. James 5:16 says, *"…The effective, fervent prayer of a righteous man avails much"*.

But we need to know that patience is a product of trust. If I trust you, your promise will mean something to me, and I won't have a problem in waiting for you when you tell me to wait. Why? Because I trust in you, and I know that you will not let me down. The best way to really know somebody is by having a close relationship with him or her. Our patience in the promises of God will emanate from our trust in Him. But we cannot trust him unless we know Him. The Apostle Paul said,

> *Yet indeed I also count all things loss for the excellence of the knowledge of Christ Jesus my Lord, for whom I have suffered the loss of all things, and count them as rubbish, that I may gain Christ and be found in Him, not having my own righteousness, which is from the law, but that which is through faith in Christ, the righteousness which is from God by faith; that I may know Him and the power of His resurrection, and the fellowship of His sufferings, being conformed to His death.*
> Philippians 3:8-10

The Bible is full of people who, by faith, patiently waited for their promise. Abraham waited for 25 years for the birth of Isaac. "*So*

Abram departed as the LORD had spoken to him, and Lot went with him. And Abram was seventy-five years old when he departed from Haran" (Genesis 12:4). And "*Now Abraham was one hundred years old when his son Isaac was born to him*"(Genesis 21:5).

David, after being anointed to be King of Israel, patiently waited for the fullness of time, (God's time) to take over the throne.

These are only two examples of many who patiently waited because they trusted God. Whatever God said to them, they believed Him, and no matter what happened they never wavered.

> *"but also to those who are of the faith of Abraham, who is the father of us all (as it is written, "I have made you a father of many nations") in the presence of Him whom he believed—God, who gives life to the dead and calls those things which do not exist as though they did; who, contrary to hope, in hope believed, so that he became the father of many nations, according to what was spoken, "So shall your descendants be." And not being weak in faith, he did not consider his own body, already dead (since he was about a hundred years old), and*

> *the deadness of Sarah's womb. He did not waver at the promise of God through unbelief, but was strengthened in faith, giving glory to God, and being fully convinced that what He had promised He was also able to perform. And therefore "it was accounted to him for righteousness".*
>
> Romans 4:16-22

How long have you been waiting for your answer? Do you trust God? Do you believe *"God is not a man, that He should lie, Nor a son of man, that He should repent. Has He said, and will He not do? Or has He spoken, and will He not make it good?* (Numbers 23:19).

Do you believe God loves you and he wants to answer your prayers? Then wait patiently. Be anxious for nothing. Just as Isaiah 40:31 says,

> *But those who wait on the LORD Shall renew their strength; They shall mount up with wings like eagles, They shall run and not be weary, They shall walk and not faint.*

You cannot live the life of faith without developing patience. Although God guarantees to fulfill everything He has promised if we will believe Him and walk in faith, He doesn't always tell us when or how. We just have to trust Him. Otherwise it will not be faith; faith is the evidence of what we hope for.

A good example that is recorded in the Bible is found in the book of Exodus. God had laid down a plan, not only to deliver His children from the bondage of Egypt, but also to give them a land flowing with milk and honey. But in the process between deliverance and the Promised Land, God took them through the wilderness. The wilderness was a place where they had an opportunity to prove God's faithfulness. I believe the wilderness was meant to force the children of Israel to learn how to depend on no one else but God. God desired the Israelites to learn to trust Him, so that when they faced bigger and fiercer enemies in the Promised Land, they would not fear. But instead of learning this lesson, they complained and grumbled.

Have you been in a situation where anybody you turned to for help turned their backs on you? Maybe you reached a point and said, "Lord on You alone I will depend. If You turn me down, I am done." That's a good place to be in! God loves us very much, and sometimes He will allow people to turn away from us, to rid us of a welfare mentality, and to teach us to trust and depend on Him and Him alone. He desires for us to be blessed so we can be a blessing. God knows there is no dignity in borrowing, but there is joy in giving.

Chapter 8

Complaining and Grumbling

Marvelous things did He in the sight of their fathers in the land of Egypt, in the field of Zoan [where Pharaoh resided].
    Psalm 78:12 (Amplified Bible)

Psalm 78 recounts for us a wonderful example of God's redemption, as well as His miraculous protection and provision. The children of Israel had just been delivered from four hundred years of bondage at the hands of the Egyptians. They had just witnessed God opening up the Red Sea to make a dry road for them, and with their own eyes, they had watched Him destroy the Egyptian army. The same passage through the sea that took them to freedom became a passage of death for their enemies. Then God gave them fresh bread every day. But this was not enough for them. They began to question God's motives and complain against Him about their situation. *"And they tempted God in their hearts by asking for food according to their [selfish] desire and appetite. Yes, they spoke against God; they said, Can God furnish [the food for] a table in the wilderness?"* (Psalm 78:18-19, AMP)

One moment they were complaining about water, and the next moment it was meat. What God supernaturally provided for them was never good enough for them! When we look at what happened, we see that God finally reached a point where He got angry with them. And He gave them what they demanded. What they thought would nourish them ended up killing them. *"But scarce had they stilled their craving, and while their meat was yet in their mouths, The wrath of God came upon them and slew the strongest and sturdiest of them and smote down Israel's chosen youth"* (verses 30-31).

And I have to tell you, my friend, as foolish as it sounds when we read about the struggles in the faith of the Israelites, sometimes we do the very same thing. Sometimes we hang on to what we have been delivered *from*, and we lose sight of what we are being delivered *to*. We think maybe it was better when we were being abused, because at least we were married. Perhaps it was better when we were doing drugs, since at least we had a few moments when our troubles seemed far away. And, on and on, we compare what we had with our current situation, because we were expecting to jump from bad to best.

But God is a loving Father, and when He delivers us from something, He will take us through a sort of "rehab" session, if I may call it that, which is meant to deal with all the pain and the lies the devil had dealt us. All the lies that we believed all those years, lies that had us believing we did not deserve better. This period is necessary because we need to be prepared for what we are going into, if we are to enjoy where we are going. If you were in an abusive relationship, you need time to recover your self-esteem and learn to trust again before you get involved in another relationship. Why? Because if you are not careful, you will carry the same pain and hurt into your next relationship, and you will end up making somebody else pay for what another person did to you—or worse—end up in another situation just like the one you've been delivered from.

The wilderness is a training ground for the battles ahead, and we will all have our own wilderness experience. The Bible tells us we should be *"casting all your care upon Him, for He cares for you. Be sober, be vigilant; because your adversary the devil walks about like a roaring lion, seeking whom he may devour"* (1 Peter 5:7-8, NKJV).

If we learn to give our cares to Him, we will not fear the roaring of the devil. But we cannot learn to trust Him enough to hand all our problems over when we are still trying to use the old methods and tactics of Egypt.

Joshua and Caleb had learned to cast their cares upon the Lord. For them it did not matter who or how long, but what mattered was what the Lord had said. That is the reason why, when the other spies feared the giants, Caleb and Joshua stood their ground believing they could defeat them. They were able to stand because of what they believed. They did not fear because they were giants themselves. They didn't see themselves as grasshoppers as the other ten did. Their faith did not come because they knew how to fight better than the others. It came because they knew the One who had promised them the land. They knew that He was able to do it. They had proved Him again and again. They had seen Him in action. But so had the others. The difference was that Caleb and Joshua would not let go of believing God.

Sometimes we need to replay previous victories when we are faced with new battles. When we remember how God took us through what we thought would finish us, our faith is built up and we gain the courage to stand and fight one more time.

In Joshua 14:6-12, we see where Caleb waited for forty years for the promise without complaining, but holding onto hope, because he knew that He who had promised is faithful.

We might feel like we are trapped in the wilderness of circumstances and situations, and the walls of helplessness may seem to be caving in on us until we either call for help or we throw in the towel and surrender. We throw tantrums and wag our fingers at God. But I ask you my friend, if you give up now, what is the alternative? I always say, "I would rather be waiting for something than nothing".

When the Israelites refused to focus on God, and got into fear, they sent Moses to meet with a holy God, whom they feared not out of reverence but out of ignorance. Since they spent their time focusing on what their flesh was lacking and what they thought they had lost by following to God into the wilderness, they were unable to see Him for who He is. They spent their time focusing on where they came from instead of where they were going. They refused to put their trust in God. And as a result, many of them died in the wilderness when they could have easily entered the Promised Land.

My brothers and sisters, if you feel like you are stagnant in your life, maybe you have not yet yielded completely to God. Maybe you are still trying to be in control. God cannot steer you if you are still holding the steering wheel. It is time to stop driving in circles, trying one relationship after another, borrowing from one to pay the other, or fighting one disease after another. It is time to turn over the wheel to the one who knows the Way. The road He chooses may be shorter or longer than you expect, but He will get you there. But if you keep on taking back the wheel after every mile traveled, you will keep finding yourself back where you started.

> *"Now the just shall live by faith; But if anyone draws back, My soul has no pleasure in him"(Hebrews 10:38), and "without faith it is impossible to please God" (Hebrews 11:6).*

Ask Abraham, when he turned over the wheel to God and trusted God's direction and driving, even when the overtaking seemed like it would lead to a cliff. But the end was prosperity, and so much blessing that the Bible tells us through him all the nations of the earth are blessed! When he was told to sacrifice his son, and he obeyed, the result was he became a friend of God. Abraham had nothing in the natural, but God made him rich, and gave him descendants innumerable—like the stars in the sky, or the sand on the seashore.

Do you want a victorious life? Then it is time for you to surrender your life to Jesus. Your graduation from the wilderness to the Promised Land depends on how close and attentive you are to the instructor, the Holy Spirit.

You need to know the One who knows the Way. Jesus said "*I am the light of the world: he that followeth me shall not walk in darkness, but shall have the light of life*" (John 8:12). It is time my friend to say, "Yes Lord, take over my life, and I will trust you." If you have been trying to fix your life for all this time, and you haven't, what have you got to lose?

Chapter 9

The Starting Point

Everyone who wants to live the good life in God must begin at the same place. The starting point to receiving God's promises is always by receiving His gift of love in the person of our Lord and Savior, Jesus Christ.

Jesus said, "*I am the way, the truth, and the life. No one comes to the Father except through Me*" (John 14:6). He also said, "*whatsoever ye shall ask in my name, that will I do, that the Father may be glorified in the Son. If ye shall ask any thing in my name, I will do it*" (John 14:13-14).

So how do you get Jesus, if He is indeed the only way to the Father? Again, we can find the answer direct from the words of Jesus. In a conversation with a man by the name of Nicodemus, as recorded in John 3:3-7, we read,

> *"Jesus answered and said to him, "Most assuredly, I say to you, unless one is born again, he cannot see the kingdom of God." Nicodemus said to Him, "How can a man be born when he is old? Can he enter a second time into his mother's womb and be born?" Jesus answered, "Most assuredly, I say to you, unless one is born of water and the Spirit, he cannot enter the kingdom of God. That which is born of the flesh is flesh, and that which is born of the Spirit is spirit. Do not marvel that I said to you, 'You must be born again.'"*

How? It is very easy to be born again. Romans 10:9-10 says,

> *"if you confess with your mouth the Lord Jesus and believe in your heart that God has raised Him from the dead, you will be saved. For with the heart one believes unto righteousness, and with the mouth confession is made unto salvation"*.

Do you believe that God loves you? Do you believe that Jesus died for your sins? Have you accepted the free gift of God--the forgiveness of your sins? If you answered yes to all these questions, then you are qualified to expect to receive answers to your prayers. But we must choose whether or not we will live out the life God has for us.

The Bible states in Deuteronomy 30: 11-20 (The Message Translation):

> *This commandment that I'm commanding you today isn't too much for you, it's not out of your reach. It's not on a high mountain—you don't have to get mountaineers to climb the peak and bring it down to your level and explain it before you can live it. And it's not across the ocean—you don't have to send sailors out to get it, bring it back, and then explain it before you can live it. No. The word is right here and now—as near as the tongue in your mouth, as near as the heart in your chest. Just do it! Look at what I've done for you today: I've placed in front of you Life and Good, Death and Evil. And I command you today: Love GOD, your God. Walk in his ways. Keep his commandments, regulations, and rules so that you will*

live, really live, live exuberantly, blessed by GOD, your God, in the land you are about to enter and possess. But I warn you: If you have a change of heart, refuse to listen obediently, and wilfully go off to serve and worship other gods, you will most certainly die. You won't last long in the land that you are crossing the Jordan to enter and possess. I call Heaven and Earth to witness against you today: I place before you Life and Death, Blessing and Curse. Choose life so that you and your children will live. And love GOD, your God, listening obediently to him, firmly embracing him. Oh yes, he is life itself, a long life settled on the soil that GOD, your God, promised to give your ancestors, Abraham, Isaac, and Jacob.

My friend, God has stated His willingness to bless you. He has outlined in His Word how He will bless you. But He has left the choice to us. We have to choose what we want. If we choose the blessings, then we have to be willing to apply and obey His principles and statutes. Those who stick to the plan will eat the good of the land.

It can no longer be our way; it has to be His way and His way alone. But His way is always the best way.

What choice are you going to make today? Will you accept this adventure of faith that guarantees you results, or would you rather keep struggling, trying to fix things on your own when you have no idea how they will end up?

Or, is it possible you are already on this journey and you find yourself crying out, when? When, Lord? Don't give up, it is better to have hope and be waiting for something, than to lose hope and fall into despair.

Remember what Hebrews 11:11 says. *"By faith Sarah herself also received strength to conceive seed, and she bore a child when she was past the age, because she judged Him faithful who had promised"*.

Choose to judge Him faithful today. It is never too late with God, and you can always count on Him.

Rev. William Kimando